I0429124

How to Be Invisible in a Digital Age:

A Newbies Guide to Protecting Your Privacy in an Electronic World

By Rebecca Robinson

Minute Help Press

www.minutehelp.com

Table of Contents

INTRODUCTION 3

CHAPTER ONE: HOW TO BE INVISIBLE IN THE
DIGITAL AGE 4
WHAT IS INVISIBILITY? 5
WHAT IT MEANS 8
A GOOD EXAMPLE 9
ADDING IT UP 12

CHAPTER TWO: HOW IDENTITY THEFT HAPPENS
....14
SCAMS AND WHAT TO LOOK FOR 16
THE HACKER AND THEIR TECHNIQUES 18
THE REALITY 22

CHAPTER THREE: HOW TO PROTECT YOURSELF..25
SPECIFIC STRATEGIES 26

CHAPTER FOUR: HOW TO DETECT IF IT'S
HAPPENED 30
SPECIFIC STRATEGIES 31
ALTERNATIVE ISSUES 33

CHAPTER FIVE: WHAT TO DO WHEN IDENTITY
THEFT HAPPENS 36
THE NECESSARY STEPS 37
BRING IN THE LAW 39
THE PHYSICAL BURDENS 40
ELECTRONIC RECOVERY 44
GOOD HABITS 46

CONCLUSION..52

Introduction

News headlines and stories from friends or colleagues can lead you to believe that you are almost defenseless against online identity theft. Though you know that your favorite websites have privacy policies, you also have no idea how they are protecting any information you give them.

The good news is that you don't have to be concerned about reliable websites when YOU take the initiative and are proactive on "your end". This guide is going to show you how identity theft and online problems can occur, and how to go about ensuring that you are as safe as possible.

One of the major tactics we'll discuss is remaining invisible, but we'll also consider how to stay safe from hackers, scammer and the rest too!

Chapter One: How to be Invisible in the Digital Age

Is it really possible to be invisible in a digital world?

Let's begin this look at invisibility in the online and digital age with one single word – <u>privacy</u>. That is the true meaning behind an interest in <u>online invisibility</u>. What is so interesting is the way that some websites or online organizations view privacy, and the widely different ways that consumers view it too.

For example, a lot of websites have an official "privacy policy" that goes into great detail about the ways the site will use the data you provide. You might read one site's privacy policy and learn that they don't share your contact information with third party advertisers, etc. Is that really privacy? No.

This guide is going to explain the <u>privacy that is desired by most consumers</u> and which ensures them that their browsing patterns are kept private, their data and banking information protected, and their computer safe from online "snooping".

Naturally, invisibility tends to be the desired domain of criminals, but let's not forget that it is also a status that people who work as free speech advocates, whistleblowers, or plain old everyday citizens looking to browse and use the Internet privately and anonymously desire too. Of course that means that in order to get the kind of invisibility we want we have to understand precisely what invisibility and/or privacy really means.

What is Invisibility?

Did you realize that the Internet was designed with protocols and systems that are the absolute opposite of private? For instance, when you use a server it is going to communicate with other servers and give out your IP (Internet Protocol) address. This is something required for servers to interact properly, but it also gives out a lot more than just a series of digits or numbers.

For example, the average IP would look something like this:

269.27.61.137

This is the style that is useable by humans, but computers have a different view known as the binary, which tends to look something like this:

11011000.00011011.00111101.10001001

Though they also have these binary forms, we only need to know that your IP address will look like a series of numbers broken up by decimal points, but these digits will tell other computers a huge amount of information.

For example, your IP might let someone else learn:

The Site From Which You Are Linking Or Your "Point Of Entry";

The User-Agent, Which Is The Program You Are Using To Browse The Web Such As Mozilla Firefox Or Internet Explorer; And

Your Operating System Such As Windows Vista, Etc.

So what, you might reasonably say, how is that an invasion of my privacy? After all, what does my point of entry on the Internet, my browsing software, and my operating system really give away?

Well, if another computer knows your point of entry, it will also tend to have access to the following details too:

City

Region Name

Latitude

Longitude

Postal code

HTTP Variables that can give access to some system information too.

Just consider that a hacker or spammer who gains access to your basic information through your online browsing might know what fonts are on your computer system, what language you use, and even determine your occupation. They can figure out if you use proxy servers by scanning the browsing history that your system information might make available as well. For instance, HTTP request variables can include things like "ACCEPT_ENCODING", "ACCEPT_LANGUAGE" and even your preference for "HTTP_CONNECTION".

Clearly, being so vulnerable to dishonest people is not a good way to surf the Internet, but it doesn't always have to be about potential criminal issues. For example, you might want to anonymously log into some sites and leave no trace of your identity. You might want to keep your browsing pattern entirely secret from sites that track IP addresses and then begin flooding you with offers, ads, and more.

What it Means

When someone is invisible in the online world, they are blocking any and all methods of tracking or spying. They tend to use some sort of encrypted connection that keeps all of their web browsing, mail, news, and chat room activities "cloaked" as well. This ensures that they are never at risk for things like identity theft, phishing, or scams of any kind. Usually it is done through the use of a "proxy server," which is something we will look at in a later chapter, but is simply a method of invisibly accessing the Internet and using most of its amazing features.

It is also a way to "work around" some common issues too. Like what? Well, let's say that your office has the social networks "blocked" and prevents employees from accessing them during their work hours. Finding a reliable proxy server can actually work around those impediments and allow people to safely bypass things like web filter systems too – and all without leaving a sign anywhere.

Again, you might ask why this matters, and we'll do a bit of a larger example to show what we mean.

A Good Example

Let's say you have a business and you want to use the Internet to "check out" the website of your primary competitor. Naturally, you don't want THEM to know you're doing this, but it is actually impossible to go in there anonymously unless you head to the local library and use their computer for hours on end.

So, you think to yourself, I'll just visit once a week and see "what's what"…that can't do much harm…right?

Wrong! Each of your visits will generate a record with the competition's site, and this is often called a "log file". Frequent visits on the same computer will begin to generate many records of this kind, and these records can allow someone to obtain the following:

The IP address information as already mentioned;

Your "WHOIS RECORD" that opens with a map showing your location, your cable or phone service company, and more;

Privacy investigation reports from third party sites; and

Browser spy information from third party sites.

This would mean that your competitor could install somewhat basic software on their own system (or hire an IT firm to install it) and learn how often you are checking them out. They can then learn a huge amount about your computer, browsing habits, etc. If, however, they got their hands on "top of the line" software, they could do even more.

For instance, when someone is attempting to just hide their IP they often forget to do the simplest tasks such as turning off cookies, JavaScript and smart updates that tend to make them very visible and trackable. While these things leave them open to all kinds of risks such as certain viruses and spyware, they can take the proper steps and still be at risk simply because they are not actually using the right sort of server.

It is usually only through very focused measures that a web user can remain invisible, and it is not all that difficult. When they are attempting to remain anonymous, invisible and private, it means that they are not likely to want people to be able to:

Collect information about requests performed in search engines;

Identify the keywords typed;

See which pages links were clicked from; and

Collect much more information about online patterns and behaviors.

Unfortunately, when you are browsing outside of a proxy server, and with your full identity and IP addressed available, you are giving competitors, and anyone else, just such an option.

Don't forget that there are also browser security holes being identified all of the time as well, and these too can lead to your identity being discovered and stolen! This demonstrates the main reason to keep up to date security on a computer too.

Adding it up

It isn't just your concerns about privacy that have come to matter. There are many global concerns about individual privacy and data integrity too. Sadly, the Internet can make things very shaky because of the way data is so readily distributed. While you might believe you are deciding what information about yourself, or your computer, to disclose, there are pieces of information you provide Internet servers with that can be available for other people without your agreement and even without your knowing.

Why put yourself in such jeopardy? There are many ways to go about defending yourself, and in the next chapters we are going to show you how identity theft occurs, how to begin protecting yourself, how to know if it has happened already, and what to do when you see that identity theft and the loss of your privacy has actually happened.

Chapter Two: How Identity Theft Happens

Before we get into the details of identity theft in the digital age, we need to make one thing very clear – identity theft can happen in the "real world" and in the computer world too. If there can be any sort of "good news" about this, it is that computer or online identity theft tends to happen far less often than the real world type, and is becoming rarer and rarer as consumers are really getting educated about the issue.

Just consider that in the real, physical world someone can do a bit of "dumpster diving" to steal personal information, can take down things like social security or credit card numbers, can watch you enter PIN numbers or passwords and use them fraudulently. They can phone you to seek information (phishing), can actually steal credit cards and banking information, and so many other illegal activities that we have no control over.

The online world, however, is limited to only a few risks, but these are things that can allow a crook to get all of your personal information and account details immediately, and this can have disastrous results. For example, a good online identity thief can use viruses, spyware, Trojan horses, worms, and other online tools and weapons to get into a computer and take as much as possible.

Naturally, implementing tactics for invisibility keeps you off of their radar. For instance, we already mentioned the use of a proxy server that keeps everything about you a very well maintained secret. This can eliminate the possibility of an online identity thief capturing any sort of data you transfer or submit over the Internet. It also prevents them from doing any "backtracking" to find out where you are or who you are!

In order to help you avoid the most common problems and to continually remain invisible while online, we'll consider the different scams, and point out what you need to look for.

Scams and What to Look For

How do you see someone "scamming" you online?
Do you envision a very well made "dummy" email
that looks like it is coming from a bank or vendor that
you have an account with? Well, that can definitely
happen. This is actually a very standard approach to
identity theft, but it can involve a lot more than you
using a bad link or handing over a bit of information.

For instance, your use of a link might launch a Trojan
Horse, a keylogger program, or a cookie stealer that
opens up your entire computer and all of the activities
you perform on it to the hacker!

Do you instead envision some sort of sneaky spying
activity that gathers credit card and personal data as
you send it over the Internet? Well…that happens too.
This is something that is actually very common when
a website is not using the most up to date servers or
security. It can also happen when a hacker does
something known as DNS poisoning or pharming,
and it is something that a lot of people don't even
realize has happened.

The thing about these two types of scams is that they
can be so easily avoided. The issue with avoiding
them is that it takes a bit of thought and effort to
ensure that you can recognize trouble when you
encounter it, and also to protect yourself from even
attracting a hacker's attention in the first place.

Remember, someone who is an identity thief is doing this as a job. This means that they have no problem spending several hours looking for as much data as possible about you. Once they have an account number, mailing address, some basic personal information, and your phone number, they can do a lot of damage.

For example, why would you list your family's names on an open Facebook wall? We all know that a mother's maiden name is one of the most common security questions. So too are pet names, high school mascots, and other personal details that tend to appear in social networking profiles. What does this mean for you? It means you MUST be aware of how the hackers operate and then keep your data private to the highest degree possible if you don't want to run the risk of scams and identity theft.

If you learn to recognize scams and security risks, and create a set of habits and behaviors that protect you from them, you can be very safe. Because the largest numbers of identity thefts are done by scammers and hackers, we'll take a look at their techniques to see how you can build the best defense.

The Hacker and Their Techniques

Today's hackers are radically different than earlier generations because they have so many programs and sneaky behaviors that can get them inside even the most protected corporate computers. Just consider that things like the major government computer systems and the major financial institutions have been hacked and lost tons of sensitive data.

A hacker "breaks into computer systems in order to steal or change or destroy information" and works to override security which results in their having "free reign" in a computer network. Once inside, they can gather data, transfer money, use credit accounts, and much more.

In modern language, hacking is done in one of three primary ways through the use of a few different techniques and strategies:

Remote Hacking – this is the scariest one in which a tech-savvy person is able to identify some sort of weakness in a remote computer system or network, get in through espionage, or via an "inside job" that delivers passwords or network information into the hands of the hacker. They then use their skills to gather information and implement their plans. This type of hacking will use;

Rogue Access Points – these are the unsecured wireless access points that a hacker can instantly break into;

Back Doors – these are ways that hackers access a network. They exploit administrative shortcuts, decipher passwords, use configuration errors, and look for unsecured dial-ups to rely on this tactic. Often, they have computerized searchers known as bots to rapidly find any weakness in a network;

DoS – this is known as a denial of service hack and is one in which hackers will actually shut down some sort of system or service, usually just for the fun of it, and usually without gaining internal access. They just flood a server with fake traffic;

Trojan horses – these are most often attached to other programs, and tend to constitute the primary method for illegally breaking into a network or individual computer. Once you open the link contained in an email (which is hiding the execution file for the Trojan Horse) you will probably lose all control of your computer system, and the hacker has access to everything from their remote location;

Sniffing – this is the true hacking that allows the individual to intercept the "packets" of information entering the computer system. This can mean that financial and personal data are literally streaming into their hands due to a security hole in the network;

Local Hacking – this is basically the same process as remote hacking with the key difference being that the hacker can actually lay their hands on the computer and use things like hard disks and thumb drives to implement their work; and

Social Networking Hacking – while we will look at the risks of using social networks too loosely a bit later, when social networking is used to describe hacking, it usually means that a hacker is working to manipulate someone in order to get data from them. This is most often a fraudulent email or communication that allows the hacker to get things like passwords, account numbers and more. These use:

Phishing scams – this is when a hacker actually tricks someone into giving up their password, account number, PIN, etc.;

Trojan horses – these are most often attached to other programs, and tend to constitute the primary method for illegally breaking into a network or individual computer. Once you open the link contained in an email (which is hiding the execution file for the Trojan Horse) you will probably lose all control of your computer system, and the hacker has access to everything from their remote location;

Keylogging – here too is a program that is secretly installed on the computer once you "fall" for a link or message. It is also due to the use of unsafe add-ons or a visit to a risky website. It will simply send a record of every single keystroke performed by you to the hacker, delivering passwords, account numbers, and everything else into their hands;

Viruses and worms – we've all been warned about opening attachments sent to us from unfamiliar email addresses, but most of us don't hesitate to open an attachment from a family member or friend. This is when we get viruses and worms that are "self-replicating" code fragments that rapidly attach themselves to everything and flood the system with "bogus" traffic such as thousands of emails, etc.

Google hacking – this is when a hacker uses the global Google search engine to find different information hidden in any unsecure directories on the web. All they do is type in a specific set of terms and wait for the results.

The Reality

Now, before you throw your hands in the air and say "I cannot possible defend myself from all of these things!" you should know that *you absolutely can*! There are many simple ways to protect yourself from these issues, which is what we cover in the next chapter. What we need you to take from this chapter, however, are the basic facts.

These facts are very simple:

Modern computers systems can be extremely vulnerable, but are particularly so when used by those unaware of the ways in which scams and hackers operate;

Understanding how they work can make it easier to avoid most of the risks present on the Internet;

Developing habits and behaviors that automatically create defensive barriers are the best ways to retain privacy and keep data secure; and

Security is never a "done deal".

This last fact is one of the most important things to remember. You can put together a very secure computer system using the latest operating software, security programs, and firewalls. You can begin using a proxy server and seeking to keep yourself as invisible as possible, AND YET in a single month's time you may discover that you are a victim of online identity theft.

How would that have happened? Unless you made sure that all of the systems and tools were as up to date as possible (meaning updating virus definitions and operating software files on a weekly or even daily basis) you may have left the back door open to a security breach. Remember that many people switch from a web browser like Internet Explorer to the Mozilla Firefox because it comes under less attack and has fewer security breaches discovered by eager hackers. There are also all kinds of new viruses and malware programs being written and released each day, and you must update your software to keep them out!

Additionally, even if your laptop had the very best of the best, if you used the wrong point of access to get on the Internet, someone could have been sitting nearby and literally plucking the information you sent right from the air.

For example, let's say that you opted to head to the local coffee shop and use their Wi-Fi access. Let's say that you also log into your email service from that spot. Unless that email service features strong encryption a good hacker with the right software will be able to grab your information. They can then start attempting to use it to log into other accounts, or they can just continue to take your messages (and even send their own on your account) for as long as they want.

The Most Basic Solution

If all of this is sending you into a panic, understand that there are three initial steps that can put you on the path to security and safety immediately:

Use security software and install all security updates;

Make sure your browser is up-to-date; and

Use online backup software

Doing these three initial steps can really help you to avoid some of the common risks coming from today's hackers, but in the next section we get into much more detail.

Chapter Three: How to Protect Yourself

Now that you might be extremely nervous about the Internet, we are going to take a few steps back and show you just how easy it can be to remain protected and secure. We just identified three of the strongest approaches:

Install all security updates - We should point out that you need to invest in a high-quality security system. Relying on the "freebies" may not get you all of the most recent virus definitions and security updates.

Make sure your browser is up-to-date - Most browsers and operating systems can be set to automatically update, and we suggest that you use this method to avoid any possible harm; and

Use online backup software - The reason that online backups are necessary is that they are often the only way to regain data if a hacker has done their nasty work on your system. It is also the one way to be sure that most of your information remains locked behind the secure door of an electronic, online vault.

The next steps will include the tactics, habits, strategies and behaviors that can be used to ensure that you remain safe in the digital world.

Specific Strategies

Never use an untrustworthy website – if your security system indicates that a website is a risk, don't go to it! For instance, if your version of security software shows a red exclamation point next to the search engine result for a site…avoid it! Sites can have all kinds of malicious code or that use your web browser by installing an "add on". This is most often the way that keylogging applications are added to a machine, and all without your permission or knowledge. The best computer security will usually identify any add on with malicious intent, and most ask you outright if you accept the add on before even beginning to download the software. Accept ONLY those that are essential and scan them before beginning any installations;

Get a virus scanning tool – your computer security system may not enable you to do "right click" scanning on files and attachments. Be sure that you have one that is installed on your system and updated on a regular basis. This is the only way to prevent yourself from downloading viruses from seemingly trustworthy sources. Additionally, NEVER open a file without first scanning for harm or threats;

Get anti-spyware and malware software – just as security programs may not have virus scanning tools, most do not have anti-spyware or anti-malware applications either. These are necessary because they prevent scammers from obtaining all kinds of useful and risky data without your knowing it. These need updates regularly too;

Install and use a firewall – this is a major way to prevent all unauthorized access between your computer and the Internet. Yes, it can cause problems when seeking to use some websites, but adjusting the individual settings for one particular site is well worth the hassle if it means that you have a major obstacle to potential scammers and hackers;

Stop and think about what you put out into the Internet – we already mentioned that scammers and hackers are more than happy to spend a lot of time digging up information. If you do a lot of social networking, but leave everything open to people who are not actually in your networks, you might as well invite a hacker into your system. We already mentioned that family names, birthdates, school information and so many other juicy tidbits appear on your social networking pages. Be aware of who you let see these details since this is a good way for someone to begin the process of identity theft;

Only go encrypted – security should be the first priority. This means that you should never work with any Wi-Fi___33 network or online service that doesn't use the latest in encryption. Certainly, you'll always look for SSL tags (that little padlock that shows a site is totally secure) and you'll double check the "http" portion of any website address to make sure that you are in a "secure" version (which changes the http to an "https") when you are submitting data, but if the information is not properly encrypted it is literally being transmitted in the clear and open air;

Pay attention to password hints and tips – most websites that ask you to select a username and a password are now also showing you if the password you select is strong or weak. If the site's little automated tool tells you that you are choosing wording that is not all that strong, listen to the advice. Try to avoid the obvious and easily guessed things like pet names, family dates, etc. Go with random assortments of terms and digits to make guessing a virtual impossibility;

Don't put your passwords into a document on your computer - A lot of people like to use spreadsheets or notepad documents on their desktop as a place to store login information, but identity thieves know this and head to this spot if and when they get into a computer; and

Consider anonymity – you can easily configure your WoW Client to remember your user name. What will this do? Let's say that a very sneaky scammer did get a keylogger on your system. With it they'd be able to get passwords, but will never be able to get your account name. This means that the information they obtain through the keylogger is useless because they have no idea how to actually login.

None of these things can be considered technically challenging, and most can be implemented in a single afternoon. Though it might cost a bit to get some of the software and programs mentioned, it will tend to make your computer perform in an optimized and completely secure manner.

This is important because one of the first signs that you have become the victim of identity theft, scammers or hackers is that you might notice a change in the way the computer performs. This could be a "slow down" from a virus or malware, and it is a good indicator that you need to take action.

Naturally, you might also see that a lot worse has occurred and that your credit cards have new charges and that your email account is no longer functioning. In the next chapter we will look at the signs that you have become a victim, and briefly address the ways to put things to a quick stop.

Chapter Four: How to Detect If it's Happened

In the last chapter we looked at strategies for preventing identity theft and online invasion of privacy from occurring. In the strategies we could have easily included the recommendation to keep an eye on your credit score in order to see if there were any radical or unwarranted changes. This is a primary strategy, but it is not as simple as it sounds.

For example, in the United States you are entitled to one free copy of your credit report each year. You get one copy from each of the main agencies (there are three – Equifax, Trans Union and Experian), but if you need a second copy you have to pay for it. You can also enroll in credit monitoring too, and that is something that we'll look at shortly.

For now, you need to understand that there are some major issues to watch for in order to detect if identity theft has occurred, and most of them can be found on the credit report. They are listed below.

Specific Strategies

When checking to see if you have been the victim of identity theft, use the following indicators:

Information changes – if your free credit reports indicate totally inaccurate information about your address, actual name, employment history, Social Security number, marital status, etc. it is a big indicator that someone got a hold of your Social Security number or has used your identity;

Mail interruptions – if you are not one of the million of "paperless" people, and you suddenly cease receiving bills, it is another indicator that something is wrong. Creditors will never just stop sending bills without your first making a request. This can be a clear sign that someone has phoned them to request a change of address, or it can mean that someone has actually stolen the physical bill from the mail and is taking additional statements to prevent you from discovering the problem straight away;

Credit cards you didn't request – whether it is a second copy of a credit card you already have or a card for an account that you did not apply for, the receipt of any unexpected credit cards is something that you need to be extremely aware of. Creditors do not take the risk of putting cards in the mail unless they think that the account holder is eagerly awaiting them at the other end;

Declines – if you attempt to use a credit card and it is declined (whether this is in person or over the Internet), don't shrug your shoulders and think you'll "give them a call tomorrow". This is because an account in good standing should never be declined. Additionally, if you are suddenly being offered the worst terms on credit accounts, such as high interest or low available balances, it could be because someone has been putting in for a lot of accounts on your credit and dragging down your rating. For instance, the more "inquiries" that appear on your credit report, the lower your credit score. This leads creditors to extend only the lowest offers and is another sign that your identity has been compromised;

New invoices – this is a "no brainer" but if you are suddenly getting bills for accounts you didn't open or for debts that you know are not your responsibility it is quite plain that you are a new victim of identity theft; and

Too many new solicitations and/or collections calls – if your phone is suddenly ringing off the proverbial hook, it is likely that someone has been passing out your phone number and your personal information. They might have triggered a wave of solicitations by accepting "offers from third parties" on a credit application or they might just have caused the calls by opening a handful of accounts and providing vendors with the means of contacting you.

Alternative Issues

Of course, this list considers only the issues most often associated with identity theft of the "predictable" or "average" kind. What about the signs of identity theft in which someone has hacked your computer?

In that case watch for:

Bizarre behaviors – one of the first indicators that you have become the victim of online identity theft is when people begin emailing you or calling you and asking you about bizarre messages you are leaving on social networks or sending out in emails. Here's a good example:

A retired woman in a small town was stopped in the post office by a friend who said, "Oh! You're back! I was going to call your daughter this afternoon". Puzzled the woman replied, "Back...I haven't been away!" Her friend looked at her and said, "But the email you sent me this morning said that you were stuck in the U.K. without the funds to get home, and asked if I could wire you money to help." The woman stood staring with a very perplexed look on her face and began to wonder if her computer had somehow been hacked.

Was the woman's machine the victim of identity theft? Absolutely! That is a classic example of the modern scam. It relies on a Trojan Horse, keylogger, or other tactic that lets the hacker obtain login information for social networks or email accounts. It then allows them to "phish" for financial contributions by sending out a very believable "SOS" through a valid person's email address. It often yields a quick profit before people realize that their accounts are being abused.

Excessive usage – if your email account is suddenly overwhelmed, and yet you know you only sent out a single message, it is likely that a virus or worm has attached itself to your account and is using it to flood a particular server, or everyone in your email address book with phishing offers or links that will help to spread the virus if opened; and

Logins that were not yours – many websites track your "last login" dates and times. It pays to watch these in order to see if your account is being entered by someone other than yourself. Services like Gmail provide this information, but so too do many billers. If you have concerns about the security of your computer, watch login information to see if you have become a victim of identity theft.

Though we just gave you even more to be aware of, it doesn't mean that you are going to have another set of hurtles and challenges. For example, if you discover that you have become the victim of identity theft, you will have to take steps to contact creditors and financial institution to make them aware of the problem. We also suggest contacting the authorities to find out how to proceed if things like a driver's license or social security card have been compromised.

Where your online actions are concerned, however, things are fairly straightforward. You are going to have to work a bit in reverse in terms of getting the system stabilized and secure, but that is the focus of the final chapter of this book.

Chapter Five: What to Do When Identity Theft Happens

The first thing to do if you discover that you have become a victim of identity theft is to take a deep breath and remain calm. There were over nine million people who dealt with the same situation over the course of the past two years alone! While some of these folks had problems because of issues in the "real world", some had their troubles because of online privacy and scams too.

The thing about all identity theft is that it tends to result in the same thing – someone uses your information to obtain credit or access financial accounts illegally. It doesn't matter is they "sniffed" data from a massive online database or if they dove into a dumpster and retrieved your monthly credit card statement – the main thing is that they are going to be causing you to literally lose a lot of your money.

The Necessary Steps

The VERY first thing we suggest you do is notify all three credit bureaus and have them put up fraud alerts. This prevents any further credit accounts or loans from being extended to "you". Remember, it is not unheard of for someone to obtain everything from car to student loans through identity theft, and they can also just as easily empty a bank account too. This means you have to alert all of the groups associated with credit approval. It starts with the three main agencies, and you can contact them at:

Equifax

P.O. Box 740250, Atlanta, GA 30374- 0241.

Report fraud: Call (888) 766-0008 and write to address above.

Web: www.equifax.com

Experian

PO Box 9532

Allen TX, 75013

Report fraud: Call (888) EXPERIAN (888-397-3742) and write to address above.

Web: www.experian.com/fraud

TransUnion

P.O. Box 6790, Fullerton, CA 92834-6790.

Report fraud: (800) 680-7289 and write to address above.

Web: www.transunion.com

Once you contact them you should also get full copies of the credit reports that they have on file – even if you need to pay for them. You will then want to consider monitoring the reports approximately every 90 days. This guarantees that nothing is going to continue to occur, and <u>if you are a bona fide victim of identity theft you may be able to get copies of the reports for free on a monthly basis</u> for the first year after the report is made and proven to be accurate.

You can also enroll in the credit monitoring services we mentioned in the previous chapter. For a range of different fees, you can begin receiving instant alerts of any activity on your credit reports, and also quarterly reports identifying issues that might be considered derogatory or problematic. If you have been a victim of identity theft, we suggest this as a very good tool in your recovery process.

Bring in the Law

The second thing to do, as we already recommended, is to communicate with local law enforcement agencies to report the issue as the full-blown crime that it is. Remember, someone may have physically stolen data or materials from you, but they also might be committing cyber-crime. Both of these activities are highly illegal and come with harsh punishments. You want to be sure that you put an end to the issue, but you also want to be sure that the criminal is caught and unable to do the same thing to other innocent people. To do this you will need all of the help you can get.

You should also know that the reports made by these agencies are one of the best forms of proof that you are not claiming anything false or misleading. It is a sad fact but there have been many people who pile up debts and then claim to be the victims of identity theft. When they make their claims to creditors and credit agencies they are asked for police reports that they cannot provide because they did not have any evidence of crime being committed. This means that obtaining documentary evidence that you discovered a crime, and acted on it, is an essential component for recovering from identity theft.

In fact, we recommend that you get an official police report with a listing of all of the accounts or websites that have been "hacked" or misappropriated by the identity thief. You can then submit that report to the Federal Trade Commission too, and they will pass this information on to investigators actively conducting national campaigns against identity theft and cyber crimes.

The Physical Burdens

Does the activity end once you have formally reported the identity theft as a crime? No, unfortunately you will have to deal with:

Problems with accounts opened fraudulently;

Problems with existing accounts;

Debt collection;

Banking and checking problems;

Fraud with the mail;

Social Security number misuse;

Driver's License misuse;

Spillover issues on family members;

False accusations; such as civil judgments based on false information; and

More!

Where these issues are concerned we suggest that you begin by closing any accounts that have been opened in your name and also any accounts that have been "tampered" with. Don't just contact customer service, however, because that will leave you open for liability. Instead do the following:

Call the creditor and ask for their security and/or fraud department. Let them know what has occurred and determine all of the fraudulent charges or activity with the agent. Then follow up in writing with them and supply supporting documentation such as police reports, etc. Be sure that the account has been closed at the time you call, but be sure to ask for written verification that the account is in dispute due to identity theft, get an identity theft affidavit from the creditor or biller, and then follow their process accordingly.

We also recommend that you immediately acquire legal help if issues such as Social Security and Driver's License number fraud have occurred. This is a major issue and is something that cannot be dealt with without proper assistance from authorities; and

We recommend you go paperless – in the modern era it is so easy to avoid so many of the physical tactics of identity theft by simply opting for paperless communications of all kinds. From bank statements and electronic filing of income taxes to paperless credit card bills and utility statements, you don't have to put that information in a situation in which it is easily stolen and abused. Naturally, this also means that you have to have a computer that is impervious to criminals, and in the next section we walk you through a recovery process for online identity theft. Before we leave the subject of paperless billing and statements, however, we do need to make one substantial comment and that is to READ EVERYTHING! Many consumers are unaware of the fact that they are victims of identity theft simply because they have gotten out of the habit of checking all of their monthly bills and statements. While it is eco-friendly to go paperless, and also dramatically safer in terms of identity theft, it also means that you could miss the fact that your credit or banking accounts are being abused because you fail to actually review the statement.

Electronic Recovery

Now we come to the somewhat technical part of the discussion and that is how to go about recovering from identity theft in terms of your online activities and your computer equipment.

Because we already explained the best ways to prevent trouble, we will just summarize the list from Chapter Four:

Never use an untrustworthy website;

Get a virus scanning tool and use it;

Get anti-spyware and malware software and use it;

Install and use a firewall;

Stop and think about what you put out into the Internet in terms of social networking, etc.;

Only go encrypted because security should be the first priority;

Pay attention to password hints and tips;

Don't put your passwords into a document on your computer; and

Consider anonymity by configuring your WoW Client to remember your user names.

We cannot know what has gone on with your personal computer in terms of the damages done by scammers or hackers, but what we can tell you that you should view any opportunity for fortifying your security and computer safety as a golden one. Yes, it might be due to a serious problem such as identity theft, but you are also going to be able to setup a system for yourself whereby this sort of thing can never happen again.

Once you have used the steps from the list above to convert your computer into the equivalent of Ft. Knox, you also have to begin establishing some habits that will help that computer to remain your first line of defense against future identity theft problems.

Good Habits

What got you into trouble with the hacker or scammer? Was it opening a link in a "friendly" email? Was it visiting a risky website even if the browser warned against it? Maybe you had no idea that a problem was occurring and you have no way of knowing how the identity theft occurred.

Regardless of the answer to the question, it is important for you to stop and consider any of the former behaviors you had in terms of Internet usage and then consider how you can possibly go about avoiding them in the future. We recommend the following considerations:

Becoming a safe surfer – this is where we'll get into a bit of conversation about those proxy servers mentioned early in the book. At the time this goes to press there are more than 40,000 proxy servers at work. They are used by more than hackers or those obsessed with anonymity and are helpful for those doing "load balancing" and data caching as well as by people annoyed by filtering or censorship. Of course, as we already stated, not all are alike and it helps to understand the following:

Open Proxies – these are HTTP and SOCKS servers that are either accessible via the Internet or left "open" by malicious individuals. The reason that people fall victim to them is that they have the advantage of working with all kinds of websites and pages because there are no modifications required to pen the page. The problem is that it is the open proxies that are so often put to use as agents in attacks. Because they are also major tools in the hands of those doing credit fraud and illegal actions, we suggest that you opt for safer options;

Web-based proxies – these are "server side" software applications that work entirely through the web browser. Usually you just go to the proxy's homepage in your standard web browser, enter the address of the site you want to visit anonymously and you are on your way! The way that they work is through a manipulation of the document or page requested, and not all are as good at it as others, but most are totally secure and a very good way to remain invisible online;

Proxy Networks – these are actual networks with layers of encryption that use the famous "peer to peer" networking. They allow the users to communicate anonymously with one another. A user operates their own equipment and count on end-users to supply a bit of their bandwidth or resources to the proxy network, but this leaves them open to a bit of danger. There are no guarantees for privacy in the networks, and they also are known for being very slow due to the shared resources; and

Proxy software – you can find subscription services that provide software that configures your web browser according to standard "proxy settings". These are not recommended because they are usually the "open proxies" which means that they leave you vulnerable to malicious users and servers.

In addition to the use of proxy servers for safer surfing, we also suggest that you make a habit of using only the most authentic and popular sites. For example, it may be appealing to shop at a little online bookstore that extends deep discounts, but if the site is full of misspellings, is not encrypted, and does not rely on SSL technologies during any transactions, it is not so charming after all. Instead, develop a list of bookmarks and make those your "go to" solutions for information gathering, shopping, bill paying, etc. Though the web should be free to surf safely, it is really wise to stick with the sites that are known to be reputable;

Savvier shopping – we just mentioned the need for encrypted transactions and reliable vendors, but we also must point out a few more indicators of whether a site can be trusted:

What is their fraud policy? For example, the massive Amazon website has very clear policies about the way they protect their customers from fraudulent use of credit cards and banking details. If something should transpire the store's policies are clearly provided as well. Any online retailer should refund the money to your account due to fraud and also ensure that all steps are taken to eliminate risks;

Look for that "https" at the beginning of the URL on the payment processing page. That guarantees that SSL is being used and that it would be very hard for someone to get the data. This also means that a valid digital certificate from an authorized issuer has been detected by your browser;

How do they communicate? All reliable vendors should have a phone number, email address, customer service form, and more. Only valid and legitimate businesses will provide ample methods of contact while the dubious vendors do not;

Stick with a single card. If you use only one credit card for all of your online transactions it will be much easier to know if it has been compromised and even easier to control the financial damages that a single identity thief has managed to accomplish;

Read your transaction statements and bills and don't just wait for the credit card statement to arrive in order to double check that the transaction was at the rate you expected. Check what the order processing emails say and print out all of the information pertaining to the transaction at the time it occurs;

Block the pop-ups. Yes, it is often challenging to run your web browser with the pop-ups disabled, but this is a good method for preventing malware, adware, spam, keylogging add-ons, and other malicious things from attacking your system. When a vendor demands that pop-ups be enabled, you should be able to cue your browser to open it the one time or always for that particular vendor alone;

Never reply to emails from vendors directly – most victims of phishing will realize that they opened an email from a vendor that they use, and followed some sort of link about their account or order. This is a classic tactic, but you should know how the vendor in question communicates. For example, the online auction site known as eBay specifically indicates that it NEVER communicates with people through emails and will do so only through their actual in-house communication system. Even then, some scammers create phishing emails that look like valid messages but which use links that are cues for malicious programs. This is one of the main reasons that browsing software, operating software, and security software updates have to be done on a very regular basis.

That's it! If you develop a computer system that is up to date, secure, and used sensibly, you will not deal with identity theft or a loss of your digital privacy. If you use the resources available wisely, you can really be sure to protect yourself in every way possible.

Whether your goal is to remain covert as you scope out the online competition, or whether you just hope to prevent an unscrupulous soul from stealing your credit information, the habits, strategies and tips provided should be able to give you every solution you need.

It all begins with knowledge – as the old saying goes "knowledge is power," and you now have all of the knowledge that you need to put up a very powerful defense against would-be identity thieves.

Conclusion

You have now gone through all of the steps necessary for identifying identity theft, preventing it from happening, and recovering from it when it does. The Internet is not a dangerous place, but there are a lot of people who use it for malicious or wrongful purposes. Because of that it is imperative to learn their tactics and motives, identify the ways to see when they are interfering with your computer equipment, and master the tactics necessary to combat them.

As you have gone through the different chapters you have probably started to think "no wonder so many people want to be invisible when they are online" and though this is a bit unfortunate, it is a fact of modern life. Operating invisibly is a good way to protect yourself from those who would seek to steal resources or interrupt your online activities for their own twisted purposes.

We hope we have helped you to develop some good plans for your own computer systems and online activities. We encourage you to do a bit of deeper investigation into things like proxy servers, security software, and the safest browsers. Things change rapidly in the world of the Internet and it is important for you to remain as well informed as your adversaries who would use the fantastic online resources for their own ill intentions.

Remember that you are not alone in the battle against an invasion of your privacy in the digital world, and even if you are already a victim of identity theft, you have a golden opportunity to create a fortress around your information. This book handed you all of the tips and tools required, and it is up to you to put them to use right away!

Good luck!

www.ingramcontent.com/pod-product-compliance
Lightning Source LLC
Chambersburg PA
CBHW060229290526
45789CB00003B/1477